ELEKTRA

Pamela Reed as Elektra with the Chorus in the CSC Repertory Ltd. production of Sophokles' *Elektra*. (*Photograph: © Paula Court.*)

SOPHOKLES

ELEKTRA

A Version by
Ezra Pound and
Rudd Fleming

INTRODUCTION BY CAREY PERLOFF

A NEW DIRECTIONS BOOK

This acting edition, first published as New Directions Paperbook 683 in 1990,
uses the text as performed by the CSC Repertory Ltd. (the Classic Stage
Company) in its 1987 production. For the guidance of directors and
performers, a literal English translation of the Greek to be spoken in the course
of the play is given at the end of the text, as is a pronunciation guide to the
transliterated sections.

All inquiries for live stage performance rights should be addressed to Samuel
French, Inc., 45 West 25th Street, New York, NY 10010; or at 7623
Sunset Blvd, Hollywood, CA 90046; or to Samuel French (Canada) Ltd., 80
Richmond Street East, Toronto, Ontario, Canada M5C 1P1.

Manufactured in the United States of America
New Directions Books are printed on acid-free paper.
Published simultaneously in Canada by Penguin Books Canada Limited

Library of Congress Cataloging-in-Publication Data
Sophocles.
    Elektra.
    (A New Directions Book)
      1. Electra (Greek mythology)—Drama.   I. Pound, Ezra, 1885–
1972.   II. Fleming, Rudd, 1908–   . III. Perloff, Carey.
PA4414.E5P68   1990   882'.01   89–14036
ISBN 0–8112–1114–2

New Directions Books are published for James Laughlin
by New Directions Publishing Corporation,
80 Eighth Avenue, New York 10011

Contents

Introduction

The age demanded an image
Of its accelerated grimace,
Something for the modern stage,
Not, at any rate, an Attic grace;

Not, not certainly, the obscure reveries
Of the inward gaze;
Better mendacities
Than the classics in paraphrase!

Ezra Pound, "Hugh Selwyn Mauberley"

In the summer of 1986, I was sitting in James Laughlin's extraordinary book-filled library in Connecticut, bemoaning the lack of playable American translations of Greek tragedy, translations that might surmount the tedious purple prose of the standard Victorians in favor of an English that was as tough and vibrant and muscular as the ancient Greek. The conversation turned to Ezra Pound, the ultimate translator. Laughlin mentioned that Pound had done a version of Sophokles' *Elektra* during the years he was confined at St. Elizabeths Hospital in Washington D.C. (1945–1958), shortly before completing his better-known translation of *Women of Trachis*. I was immediately fascinated: the *Elektra* was one of the tragedies I was most interested in directing, and one of the least well-translated of Sophokles' works. The original manuscript of the Pound version was, I discovered, owned by Omar Pound (it has subsequently been sold to the Princeton University Library, where it now resides in the Department of Rare Books and Special Collections), but a duplicate existed in the Beinecke Library at Yale, and Laughlin had a Xerox himself. He pulled it out of a drawer and gave it to me, with the caveat that it was probably an unfinished translation; Pound had never sought to have it published.

I returned home with Pound's text and set to work with my Loeb Greek text of *Elektra*, reading the two side by side. What astonished me immediately about Pound's version, which was not in the least unfinished, was its remarkable fidelity to the Greek. Needless to say, "fidelity" for Pound had nothing to do with literal semantic sense; Pound *sounded* Greek to me. "Don't translate what I said, translate what I meant to say" was his credo, and it seemed clear from the start, at least in my mind, that Pound had translated what Sophokles "meant to say." Pound's version of *Elektra* was rhythmically complex, dissonant, often hilarious, and yet surprisingly moving. It held within it such a heartfelt portrayal of the title character as to suggest that Elektra was not just a Greek princess to Pound but one of the "personae" with whom he most closely identified.

Prior to his adaptation of *Elektra*, which was written in 1951, Pound had shown relatively little interest in Sophokles; indeed, in his critical writings Sophokles is almost never mentioned. His interest at the time of the *Elektra* translation seems to have been piqued by a classicist from the University of Maryland, Rudd Fleming. Pound and his wife, Dorothy, had become friendly with Fleming through Fleming's wife Polly, a Laforgue enthusiast who had shared her translations with Pound over many visits to St. Elizabeths, where Pound was confined for thirteen years. On one visit, Rudd Fleming brought Pound his own rendering of the Tutor's central speech in *Elektra* (pages 29-31) in which the clever "Paidegogos" weaves a false tale about Orestes' death to a grieving Elektra and a rejoicing Klytemnestra. Fleming encouraged Pound to try his hand at this superb bit of false "logoi," and Pound leapt in with relish, coming up with a parody of Irish brogue that perfectly encapsulated the blarney of Sophokles' sly messenger:

> And the umpires ranged 'em up as the lot fell
> and they sounded off with the brazen horn
> shakin' the reins and a-lickin' the horses
> and a-yellin' till you couldn't hear over the plain
> and the track wuz narrow, the lot of 'em drivin' togedder
> and a-lammin' the horses, each one tryin' to get out of

the bunches
and the wheels a-rollin', and the horses a-snortin'
and their sweat spattered over the cars,
and their breath steamin' on the droivers in front of 'em
and Orestes come round at the turn . . .

The verbal virtuosity and sense of suspense, so precisely executed in the Greek through escalating rhythm, is palpable in Pound's version. Indeed, by imbuing the language of the Paidegogos with the brogue of an archetypal Irish horse trader/hustler/bookie/quick-talking con man, Pound found a fascinating contemporary persona for the Tutor, whose verbal deception destroys before it can heal.

The power of language to deceive was an obsession with Pound, particularly in his role as translator. He was convinced that the act of carrying over meaning from one language to another was by definition an act of betrayal. This notion of verbal deception lies at the core of Sophokles' *Elektra,* in which characters are constantly revealing or concealing themselves through the use of verbal "masks," masks which often prove very dangerous indeed. Finding English equivalents for these verbal deceptions allowed Pound to experiment with the huge range of dialects and English idioms at his command. One of the most potent examples of this, aside from the Paidegogos' speech, is the smooth-talking cockney mask Pound created for Orestes when Orestes first confronts Elektra: "Eh, can any of you ladies/ tell me: did we hear right and/ are we gettin' to where we wanted to come to?" The tough verbal mask is so impenetrable that Elektra is completely deceived, and her grief at Orestes' false tale is heartbreaking.

Each verbal gesture, each rhythmic change, is carefully articulated in the Pound. With Fleming as his Greek consultant, Pound worked through the play section by section; his tools were the Jebb Edition *Opera* Part VI, and a metronome. The two men took turns reading the Greek aloud, discerning each rhythmic choice and then devising English equivalents. It was clearly the *sound* far more than the literal, semantic, or psychological sense that Pound tried to approximate. For there are sounds in ancient Greek (such as *pampsuxos,* "all-breathing") that appear in no other language; a good translation had to take these sounds into account if the dramatic sense of the whole was to come through. Pound had objected to T. S. Eliot's recently produced *The Cocktail Party,* a version of Euripides' *Alcestis* so far removed from the Greek that the majority of its audiences had no idea they were seeing anything other than a British drawing room comedy. There was no reason, Pound said, for ancient Greek to sound like rarified British English. As he had written in 1912 of H.D.'s "Hermes of the Ways": "It is in the laconic speech of the Imagistes . . . objective—no slither—direct—no excess of adjectives. No metaphors that won't permit examination. It's straight talk—*straight as the Greek.*"

As a translator, certain sections of the *Elektra* appealed to Pound immediately, while certain parts seem to have been left to Fleming to "fill in" in the same vein. Evidently the text was passed back and forth between the two of them many times. The original copy is sprinkled with Pound's impertinent questions and commentary, often rhetorical, such as his query about Klytemnestra: "How vulgar ought she to be? The vulgarity, lack of emotional control are the mess Elektra and her brother have to clean up, so I don't suppose she can be too vulgar, as long as the vulgarity remains dramatic." Of course he proceeded to make Klytemnestra as unspeakably vulgar as possible, to great dramatic effect.

> Out here again making trouble, might have known it
> now Aegisthus' not here,
> he keeps you from making dirt on the family doorstep.
> He's away and you pay no attention to me.
> You've shot off a lot of brash talk
> to a lot of people,
> a lot more than was so
> about how forward I am, how unjust
> insulting you and your gang.
>
> Nobody ever insulted me? Eh?
> Bad? Eh?
> Well I've heard 'em from you often enough
> just as bad.

Pound's Klytemnestra is a salty American shrew, by turns lascivious, seductive, and ruthlessly vindictive, but also refreshingly honest and unfailingly *real*. How pale she looks by comparison in her standard Loeb Classic incarnation:

> So once again I find thee here at large,
> For he who kept thee close and so restrained
> thy scandalous tongue, Aegisthus, is away.

No thee's and thou's for Pound's Klytemnestra; she truly makes Elektra fear for her life.

For a writer who had tried his hand at playwriting only in adaptations of the Japanese Noh plays, Pound's sense of the dramatic in *Elektra* is uncanny. Most translators of Greek tragedy tend to forget that, as full of poetry and myth as these plays were, they were primarily successful because they *played*, because they were eminently actable on stage to please a wide and diverse audience. Rarified lyrics and distorted syntax do not play, and Pound had no more tolerance for floridity on stage than he had for it in poetry. "Poetry must be as well-written as prose," he insisted. "Its language . . . departing in no way from speech save by a heightened intensity (i.e. simplicity) . . . no book words . . . no hindside beforeness, no straddled adjectives (as 'addled mosses dank') . . . nothing that you couldn't, in some circumstances, in the stress of some emotion, actually say."

Pound's sense of the dramatic idiom of American speech and of the idiosyncracies of human behavior were particularly well-suited to the *Elektra*, a play whose situation and linguistic expression bear a strange resemblance to Pound's world in St. Elizabeths. *Elektra* is the story of a woman obsessed with her own past. The play explores the madness of incessant "remembering," the terror of being unable to forget the past in a culture or household in which history is being deliberately erased:

> Split his head with an axe as
> a woodcutter splits a billet of oak,
> and that killed him
> and nobody else in this house seems to mind.
> Well I'm not going to forget it
> and all the stars can shine on it, all of them
> destiny

> tears of hate
> all flaming rips
> of the stars
> tide
> and the day can look on it.
> I won't stand it and just keep quiet.

Is this the language of the only truly moral person in the play, or of a madwoman? The question of Elektra's sanity is one that has fascinated critics and theatergoers since Sophokles first presented her in 431 B.C. It clearly fascinated Pound, who not long before, at his sanity hearing in Federal Court, had pled insanity to avoid standing trial for treason. The legal definition of insanity is slippery at best, and the paradox of using legalistic jargon to probe the stability of an anguished person's mind was not lost on Pound. Ironically, it was the need to prove his own insanity that made Pound hesitate to publish the *Elektra;* he thought a man sane enough to translate Greek might be considered sane enough to stand trial for treason.

The fine line between sanity and insanity is made clear in Pound's version of the "trial" scene between Elektra and Klytemnestra over Agamemnon's murder. To Elektra, Klytemnestra and Aegisthus's murder of Agamemnon is a bleeding sore that must be cauterized by Klytemnestra's death if the household is to be healed again. To Chrysothemis, it is worth giving up vengeance against her mother in exchange for the hope of baubles and babies in the future. To Klytemnestra, the murder of Agamemnon was justified by Agamemnon's prior "sacrificial" murder of Iphegenia and thus merits no further retaliation, despite her daughter's mad obsession. Words against words, true *logoi* versus false *logoi,* sanity versus madness—Pound revelled in these linguistic manipulations. But he also had a clearly emotional reaction to Elektra's plight, to the tragedy of being deemed "mad" for refusing to forget. His Elektra is a caged prisoner, sleeping in dark corners in her mother's house, only venturing into the sunlight (*"Oo Phaos agnon!"*) when Aegisthus is away and cannot torment her.

Without attempting to make Pound into a similar type of tragic figure, his experience at St. Elizabeths bears at least superficial resemblances to the Elektra story. He had returned to America a prisoner after having been held in a cage built of aircraft landing mats in the Army's Disciplinary Training Center in Pisa. In his captivity the wreckage of World War II filled his head ("No wonder my head hurts," he said. "All Europe fell on it; when I talk it is like an explosion in an art museum.") Flown to Washington after his indictment for treason, Pound found an America he hardly recognized. It was a country obsessed not with the horrors of the past but with the pleasures of the present: with babies, big cars, jazz, and consumerism—a world his bejewelled Chrysothemis would have understood perfectly. Committed to St. Elizabeths after the court found him to be of unsound mind, he was placed first in the criminal section of the hospital and then moved to the senile ward, where he lived in a dark little cubicle and received guests behind a Chinese screen in the main corridor. He was allowed out into the daylight of the hospital grounds only a few times a week. The prevalent dark/light imagery of Sophokles' *Elektra* obviously struck a resonant chord.

During the afternoon visiting hours an extraordinary range of people came to pay court to him: old friends, famous and unknown poets, professors and translators such as the Flemings, and a faithful band of young disciples made up largely of eccentric literary riffraff and believers in his bizarre theories of monetary reform and politics. It was a babel of discordant but uniquely *American* voices. I suspect that when it came time for Pound to tackle the Choral sections of the *Elektra*, it was these idiomatic, ever-changing voices that he evoked, along with the pragmatic tough talk of the soldiers, prisoners, and guards in the camp at Pisa. Pound's choral ladies are not abstract ethereal beings, but earthy, well-meaning, mundane types that one might find volunteering in the local library or on the ward at St. Elizabeths. They come to bear witness, not to effect change. Their language is filled with the idiomatic American diction that Pound was so fascinated by, particularly now that he was hearing it spoken again on native soil: throughout their speech we find echoes of black American speech, new slang, film talk, song lyrics, and the strange speech of the mad with whom he lived.

ELEKTRA

The relationship of the Choral Ode to dialogue and stichomythia in Greek tragedy is one of the greatest challenges for any translator of Greek. Those who get the poetry of the Chorus right tend to miss the pungent colloquialisms of the dialogue, and vice versa. In his translation of the *Elektra,* Pound comes up with many solutions to this critical problem. One in particular seems remarkably simple on the face of it: he leaves many of the Choral sections of the play in the original Greek, juxtaposing the Greek text with a parallel English translation. For example, in urging Elektra to cease her lamentation for Orestes, the Chorus begins with colloquial American pragmatism:

> But you won't get him out of black hell
> By praying and groaning,
> you destroy yourself with too much of it,
> no harm to let up for a little.

Then Pound writes on the manuscript "emphatic and explicit with meaning to ram it in" and gives the Chorus three lines of transliterated Greek:

> ALL OUTOI TON GEX AIDA
> PANGKOINOU LIMNAS PATER ANSTASEIS
> OUTE GOOIS OUTE EUXAIS
> Nothing to be DONE about it.

What is striking about the Greek lines are the monosyllables and repeated strong stresses with which Sophokles hammers home the Chorus' insistent scolding:

As translator, Pound clearly realized that this pounding effect was far more potent in the *quantitative* prosody of Greek than in the *accentual* prosody of English. He wanted to preserve the colloquial, "real life" quality of the Greek without losing its insistent pulse. The passages of slangy English thus took care of the former, while the juxtaposition with the original Greek preserved the latter. By introducing the use of Greek within a colloquial English context,

Pound also created a complex verbal system that only Elektra and the Chorus share.

In Pound's version, the Greek thus becomes a form of private communication between the Chorus and Elektra, capable of expressing emotions and reactions whose *sound* is as important as their semantic meaning. "The sum of human wisdom is not contained in any one language," Pound had written in *The ABC of Reading*, "and no single language is capable of expressing all forms and degrees of human comprehension." The use of ancient Greek embedded in the English translation of the *Elektra* may thus be seen not as a translator's evasion but as a potent device to get us to listen more carefully to the nuances of Elektra's grief, and to make that grief palpable in a sonic sense on the stage. The two languages serve to reinforce each other: the rhythmic electricity of the Greek next to the reassuring familiarity of the English. This act of slipping from one language into another among close friends or family members is a distinctly American phenomenon. An Italian-American mother will lapse into her native tongue when upbraiding or comforting her child, only to return in the next breath to Brooklynese English. Indeed, if American English is, as Pound clearly believed, the repository of many disparate languages, then as Americans we can achieve the richest means of expression on stage by introducing fragments of as many of those languages and dialects as possible, tapping the "primal memory" of the audience on multiple levels.

Pound's attention to the sound and rhythm of his characters' speech is particularly important because of the way language itself functions in the *Elektra*. It must be remembered that *words (logoi)* are Elektra's only weapon, her only source of active vitality. Although her overwhelming desire is to kill her mother, all she can do is *talk* about it; it is Orestes who accomplishes the deed. The play is split between *logoi* and *erga*, between words and deeds, between those who live by *testifying* and those who live by *doing*. This linguistic split is symptomatic of a basic dichotomy emphasized by Sophokles, the male/female dichotomy that was so marked in ancient Greek culture.

The clearest example of this dichotomy occurs at the beginning of the play. Sophokles' version of the story opens not with a speech by his heroine but with the terse iambic dialogue of Orestes and his Tutor. Speaking of the Oracle's instructions to him, Orestes says: "DOLOISI KLEPSAI KAIROS ENDIKOS SPHAGAS." ("By treachery, steal the opportunity to strike the avenging blow.") The words *kleptai* (to steal) and *kairos* (the right time, profit) are repeated words among the men in the house of Atreus, along with *kerdos* (gain), *dolos* (treachery), *kleos* (honor) and *kruptein* (secrecy). Pound clearly loved the hard repeated "k" sounds of these words and the terse, laconic syntax into which Sophokles had placed them. Accordingly, he gave Orestes the language of an American cowboy, active, swaggering and quick on the draw. In translating the Greek phrase quoted above, Pound's Orestes says, "Dont start a war,/ take a chance, do it yourself:/ Kinky course, clean in the kill." Sophokles' alliterative "k" sounds thus find their way into Pound's tough American English. In both cases, the language serves to reveal a character with no sentiment, no doubt; Orestes has come home to avenge his father and reclaim his inheritance, and he's ready to take action *immediately:*

> This is what we're agoin' to do,
> listen sharp and check up if
> I miss any bullseyes . . .
> you nip into this building, find out everything that's
> being done there, and keep us wise to the lot of it. Snap.

Into this deed-oriented, iambic male world comes a cry: "OO MOI MOI DUSTENOS!" and then "OO PHAOS AGNON." From out of the darkness crawls Elektra, wailing in Greek. Immediately we are in a different world. Elektra's language is beyond prose. She lives in the *agones* of early Greek tragedy, and her language is personal, volatile and expressive. She constantly reaches for images, sounds, and allusions that will give shape to a grief that has no end, to a life with no way out, and when English fails to express her feelings, she uses Greek. Locked in her mother's house, her only recourse is to *make noise,* to speak out, against all odds. ("They've got the power," she says. "All I can do is yammer/ and make too much noise.") Words are Elektra's weapons, and lamentation her occupation. It must be remembered that women in ancient Greece had no access to public life. They were not privy to political debate, legal disputes, or public discourse, so their language took on a distinctly personal form. Pound, who was constantly frustrated by his limited access to civic power, understood this phenomenon well. He would have liked nothing better than to discourse with the political powers at hand, but repeatedly ended up concocting his own private language instead.

Sophokles' clear distinction between public and private language in the *Elektra* is rarely evident in the work of translators of this play, but Pound grasped and indeed heightened this linguistic dichotomy. Not only did he introduce Greek into Elektra's vocabulary, but he found a poetry for Elektra that stands in sharp contrast to Orestes' firm masculine prose.

OO PHAOS AGNON
      Holy light
Earth, air about us,
      THRENOON OODAS
      POLLAS D'ANTEREIS AESTHOU
tearing my heart out
when black night is over
all night already horrible
been with me
my father weeping
there in that wretched house
weeping his doom.

From Sophokles' text, Pound plucks image clusters which stand as discrete entities in Elektra's speech, one piled upon the next. There are images of darkness and light, fragments of memory, repeated sounds, and most of all the jagged stresses of someone crying, gasping for breath: "Aĺl nght alréady hórrible/béen with me . . ." Whenever a sound or an emotion cannot be expressed well in English, Pound brings back the Greek, not only during sequences of lamentation but during sequences of great defiance: "I wont stand it and just keep quiet/ ALL' OU MEN DE/ LAEXOO THRENOON." The repeated long stresses of the Greek hammer out a counterpoint to the English phrase before it, giving the actress great range and texture to work with in creating the role of Elektra.

Elektra's language, in the Pound version, is also marked by its *condensation,* often achieving great emotional richness through economy of expression. For example, when Elektra finally realizes that the mysterious stranger before her is in fact her long lost brother Orestes (page 57), the Greek gives her four lines, which literally translated read: "Oh child, child of my best-loved body, now you have seen exactly, you have come to be possessed of what you most yearned for." In Pound, an overcome Elektra whispers six short words: "Heart, heart, heart, thou art come." All the verbs are gone except the verb "to come"; Pound's Elektra expresses the inexpressible in as few words as possible.

To enumerate the verbal inventions Pound discovered while translating *Elektra* would be beyond the scope of this introduction. Not only did this exploration of Greek tragedy put to use many of the verbal and rhythmic experiments of a lifetime of writing, but it stretched Pound in new directions. For example, in the crucial section of the play in which Elektra mourns over the supposed ashes of her dead brother, Pound created a pulse of grief unique in his canon, which he set off with the title "Elektra's Keening":

> All that is left me
> my hope was Orestes
> dust is returned me
> in my hands nothing, dust that is all of him,
> flower that went forth.

The condensation, synecdoche, imagistic precision and extraordinarily simple repeated rhythm make this section of the play deeply moving, particularly in contrast to the abrupt cockney slang of Orestes with which it is juxtaposed. Later, when Pound wished to highlight Elektra's delight at convincing her sister Chrysothemis to side with her against her mother, he created a sort of rap rhythm that puts us right onto the streets of contemporary America:

> You can say that I never guess right,
> a born fool without second sight,
> that my head was never screwed tight,
> but if Justice don't win just this once
> I'm a dunce

How then do we take this rich amalgam of languages and put it onto the American stage? Each director must solve this problem in his or her own way. But let me try to describe very briefly some of the choices we made for the production I directed in November, 1987, at CSC Repertory, the Classic Stage Company, in New York.

I began with the notion that the production, like the translation, had to build a bridge between two clearly evoked cultures: ancient Greece and contemporary America. While Pound's translation of *Elektra* is indisputably American in its language, rhythm, and sensibility, Pound did *not* attempt to set the play literally in 1950's Washington, in the way that Eliot had set his version of *Alcestis* in contemporary Britain. We are in Argos, yet we are also at St. Elizabeths. Elektra is a Greek princess, yet she is also a *persona* of Ezra Pound. The tensions between varying cultural sources inform the entire translation, and we tried to express these tensions in every aspect of the production so that Pound's version was not watered down into "palatable Greek tragedy" as we have come to expect it.

We began by designing a set which followed the basic line of an ancient Greek stage: the deep orchestra, the huge back wall with the ominous portal, the chiseled hard white lines of ancient stone. But our set was made of concrete, not marble, and running across the "orchestra" on a long diagonal line was a chain-link fence, the fence that kept Elektra locked into her "yard" except when Aegisthus was away. The production at CSC happened to take place during one of the many bomb scares at the American Embassy in Beirut, and the newspaper photographs of the barricaded embassy with huge concrete pylons abutting barbed wire fencing must have been somewhere in our visual consciousness as we designed the set. We had also looked at pictures of the human "cages" at the Detention Center in Pisa, and of the lawns and high brick walls of St. Elizabeths, all of which helped to shape the scenic design for this frighteningly contemporary story of a woman held hostage in her own home. Our main goal was to keep the visual elements as clean and hard-edged and precise as the language. Both in terms of scenery and costumes, we tried to evoke the multiple cultures and epochs in evidence in Pound's script. The folds of fabric of Elektra's dress fell like Greek sculpture, but the Chorus sat on 1950's metal porch furniture. A great deal was made of stark white light and shadow, since dark/light imagery is one of the crucial threads in both the Sophoklean and Poundian *Elektras.*

One of the most difficult visual problems to solve in any production of Greek tragedy is the placement and use of the *altar.* Scholars are still debating its exact location on the ancient stage. The altar is significant in *Elektra* because each character uses it to make libations and prayers to gain his or her own particular goal. Yet in this world of American slang, Irish brogue, and cockney strutting, we couldn't mimic an ancient slab of marble. We chose instead to dig a hole in the stage floor and cover it with a heavy metal grate, like a sewer grate on an urban American street. Out of the grate shone a murky green light evoking both the dank underground of any modern city and, more abstractly, the vengeful underworld of the ancient Furies whose imminent presence is constantly felt in the play. We opened the production with Orestes pouring a libation of milk through the rusted grate into the green depths below, while Wayne Horvitz's jazz score pulsated over the speakers. As the play unraveled, the darkness inside the grate became more and more alive and ominous, holding within it the secrets of each member of the family. Finally at the end of the play, after the murder of Klytemnestra, a bright shaft of light shot out through the grate, illuminating Elektra's slightly mad face as she knelt before the altar with an armful of wheat. Her victory was complete, but at what price?

When casting the play, I again focused on the fact that what makes Pound's version universal is its use of languages from many cultures and ethnicities. I wanted the actors on stage to represent the cultural diversity of contemporary American life in the same way. Thus Elektra was played by Pamela Reed, her bleached blonde hair flashing in the white light, and Orestes was played by African-American actor Joe Morton in cowboy boots and blue jeans. Aegisthus was played by a Hispanic actor, Jaime Sanchez, and Klytemnestra was played by Nancy Marchand as an elegant, alcoholic WASP. The plurality of the cast gave this *Elektra* an American immediacy without having to place the action literally in the contemporary United States.

The performance style sprang from the kinetic, energetic, frontal attack of the language. Reed's Elektra literally climbed the walls and shook the chain-link fence, yet many of her physical poses were derived right from the Greek. We examined dozens of Greek vase paintings of Maenads in ecstacy while choreographing the recognition scene between Elektra and Orestes. The actors were made acutely aware of changes in rhythm from line to line, and of the need to use the language as an active tool.

The most difficult decision was how to handle the end of the play. From the murder of Klytemnestra onwards, the text is very abrupt. Elektra abandons her lyrical language and in a frightening reversal begins to speak in the male jargon of Orestes: "Don't let him get a word in,/the brute's caught, What good's a half hour?/Kill him. Kill him." Aegisthus is trapped; the plot unfolds at breakneck speed. Finally, in the last five lines, the Chorus explodes as if letting their breath out for the first time in the play:

> My god, it's come with a rush!
> DELIVERED, DELIVERED
> SWIFT END
> SO SOON
> TE NUN TELEOOTHEN.

But by then Elektra herself is silent. This paragon of verbal energy finally has no more words. The murder accomplished, her *raison d'être* has disappeared. In the echoing silence of the final blackout, a huge question looms in the air: NOW WHAT? Will the Furies arrive to take their revenge, or have Elektra and Orestes been truly victorious in ending the cycle of destruction? The deliberate ambiguity of the Sophoklean ending must have been frightening for Pound. Like Elektra at the end of the play, Pound's life at the time he did this translation, and indeed his whole aesthetic embodied in the still-incomplete *Cantos,* hung in the balance. Too many words had been spoken; soon it would be time for silence. The question remained to be asked: was Elektra's courageous stance a victory or ultimately a tragic, futile act in the face of the inevitable march of history?

The image of the double-headed axe is so prevalent in the play that one can't help but fear another cycle of revenge: what strikes one way must come back. Certainly in Pound's translation, the sheer thrust of verbal energy leading up to the end of the play is breathtaking, and the exhilaration of an action well done leaves us with a feeling of victory for Elektra. But the weight of her action is even more ambiguous in the Pound than in the Sophokles. For in her Greek context, Elektra was part of a world view that believed in catharsis and purification. It was possible that the murder of Klytemnestra would result in another cycle of revenge, but ultimately the Greek audience knew that through adjudication the House of Atreus would be cleansed. That was the ritual power of tragedy. In the post-war world of Ezra Pound, on the other hand, there is no such certainty. For in a culture of fragments such as our own, a culture in which the shared moral or religious beliefs of old Europe have been blown to bits, can there ever be a tragic act again, or are we only left with an ironic gesture? Can one create true catharsis out of broken puzzle pieces? Is "ritual purification" even a possibility?

The best that Pound's Orestes can promise Elektra after the murder of Klytemnestra is that, "You won't have any more trouble with mother." This line caused immediate laughter in the audiences that saw the production in New York: a laughter of horror, granted, but laughter nonetheless. Indeed, an audience watching Pound's *Elektra* is constantly torn between tears and laughter. For tragedy had turned into black comedy by the time Pound tackled the *Elektra.* Absurdism was around the corner. Pound's translation is as much about the end of Europe as he knew it (the culture that revered and believed in Sophokles) as it is about the tragedy of Elektra herself. So many broken statues, broken promises, lost languages, fragments of thought. Could anything ever "cohere" again? Probably not.

The tragic act is an act of a past culture, never to be repeated with the same effect. Yet this does not mean that we cannot translate or produce tragedy for the modern stage. It means we must acknowledge at the outset that we are no longer a homogeneous culture like ancient Greece. We no longer share rituals which, if collectively experienced, will leave us collectively cleansed. At best, we are gatherers of potsherds, piecing bits of a destroyed world together. It is the tension between these multiple fragments and the unity they once evoked that creates the drama of Pound's *Elektra*. The attempt to make a perfect replica of a once beautiful pot is clearly doomed, and Pound knew it. But in recombining the scattered pieces, one can try, as Pound did over and over again, to make something NEW out of the rubble.

Carey Perloff
Artistic Director
CSC Repertory Ltd.
(Classic Stage Company)
August, 1989, New York

ELEKTRA

Dramatis Personae

ELEKTRA	daughter of Agamemnon and Klytemnestra
ORESTES	son of Agamemnon and Klytemnestra
KLYTEMNESTRA	Queen of Argos, widow of Agamemnon
CHRYSOTHEMIS	sister of Elektra and Orestes
AEGISTHUS	Klytemnestra's lover and accomplice
TUTOR	Orestes' rescuer
CHORUS	of Mycenaean women
PYLADES	silent friend to Orestes

Elektra was presented by CSC Repertory Ltd. (The Classic Stage Company) at the CSC Theatre in New York City on November 1, 1987. It was directed by CSC Artistic Director, Carey Perloff; scenic design was by Donald Eastman, costume design by Candice Donnelly, and lighting design by Frances Aronson; original music and sound design was by Wayne Horvitz. The production stage manager was Dara Hershman, the casting director Ellen Novack and the production manager was Jeffrey Berzon. The cast, in order of appearance, was as follows:

TUTOR	William Duff-Griffin
ORESTES	Joe Morton
PYLADES	Keith Overton
ELEKTRA	Pamela Reed
CHORUS	Lola Pashalinski
	Isabel Monk
CHRYSOTHEMIS	Veronica Cartwright
KLYTEMNESTRA	Nancy Marchand
AEGISTHUS	Jaime Sanchez

Scene: at Mycenae, in front of Agamemnon's palace

TUTOR:
 Well, here's where your father landed when he
 got back from the Trojan war, this is where you
 wanted to come to;
 Old Argos over there
 where the gad-fly chased Miss Inachus,
 and that's the Lukeum, named after the wolf-god,
 the wolf-killer, market place now;
 and Hera's church on the left
 everybody's heard about that.
 Down below there: Mycenae,
 center of the gold trade,
 and Pelops' palace, the throne room,
 where the dirty murder was done.
 That's where I picked you off your dad's
 bloody body,
 that is to say your kind sister
 did, and give you to me to take off and raise
 like a proper avenger.

 And now, Orestes, it's up to you
 and your dear friend Mr. Pilades, stranger in these parts.

3

Get goin' quickly.
Sun's risin', birds are singin',
stars going down, darkness broken.
Get going before people start moving about
and be clear in your own minds what you're up to.

ORESTES:
All right, Old Handy,
you sure have stuck with us
like a good ole horse rarin' for battle,
urgin' on and keepin' right forward
up in front every time.
This is what we're agoin' to do,
listen sharp and check up if
I miss any bullseyes.

When I went off to the Pythoness
to ask about doin' right by my father
Phoebus answered:
Don't start a war,
take a chance, do it yourself:
Kinky course, clean in the kill.

Now as that's the oracle we heard
the first chance you get
you nip into this building, find out everything that's
being done there, and keep us wise to the lot of it. Snap.
Nobody'll recognize your old block
after all these years, under all this herbage.
Make your cock-crow.
You've come here from their best pal Phanoteus
first time you've ever been out of Phocia.
Swear that Orestes was killed in a chariot race
at the Pythians. Put in the details.

We'll go to Dad's tomb as ordered
with libations an' all my pretty curls

we'll bring back that nice brass urn
we hid in the underbrush
to back up the yarn that I'm dead
and buried
and this dust all that is left of me.
They'll like that.
I don't mind being dead that way
if I can live on in honor.
I don't suppose the lie will ruin our luck,
not the first time a wise guy
has said he was dead
in order to get a warm welcome.

Earth of the fatherland
bless the roads we have come by
for the old home and this clean up,
the gods are in me to do this,
clean the old home
that I be not sent back into exile dishonored
give me back the heritage
that I bring back the old rule of abundance
and make it solid.

Nuff talk. Get in there, old buck, and
keep steady
and we'll go now
and watch for the moment—
time, time
best leader men have.

ELEKTRA:
Oh, oh, I'm so unhappy.
IOO MOI MOI DUSTAENOS

TUTOR:
Some slavey howling inside there.

ORESTES:

   Poor Elektra, might be,
   wanna stay and listen?

TUTOR:

   Certainly not. Get our bearings first
   as Loxias ordered. Holy water to wash up
   the tomb-stone.
   That's the way to win out.

(TUTOR *and* ORESTES *exit*)

ELEKTRA:

   OO PHAOS AGNON
                  Holy light
   Earth, air about us,
             THRENOON OODAS
             POLLAS D'ANTEREIS AESTHOU
   tearing my heart out
   when black night is over
   all night already horrible
   been with me
   my father weeping
   there in that wretched house
   weeping his doom.
   Not killed abroad in the war
   but by mother and her bed-boy Aegisthus.
   Split his head with an axe as
   a woodcutter splits a billet of oak,
   and that killed him
   and nobody else in this house seems to mind.
   Well I'm not going to forget it
   and all the stars can shine on it, all of them,
   destiny
             tears of hate
             all flaming rips
             of the stars

tide
and the day can look on it.
I won't stand it and just keep quiet.
                    ALL' OU MEN DE
                    LAEXOO THRENOON
You can't stop the nightingale crying, for her young,
or me
on the porch,
let everyone hear it,
Hell and Persephone
                    OO DOOM AIDOU
OO KHTHONI HERMAE, OO Queen of Avenging,
O Vengeance,
Hear me,
ye that watch over shed blood,
over murder, over the usurping of beds.
CURSE, and hear me
god seed, ye Erinnys, of doom
aid and defend us, avenging our father's death
                    HAI TOUS ADIKOOS THNAESKNONTAS
                     HORATH
                    HAI TOUS EUNAS HUPOKLEPTOMENOUS
                    ELTHET ARAEXATE

(*sinks onto step*)

and
send me my brother
I can do no more on my own
this
grief is too heavy.

CHORUS:
Poor Elektra
                    OO PAI PAI DUSTANOTATAS
you had a curse for a mother
                    ELEKTRA MATROS TIN AEI

7

and are withered with weeping
        TAKEIS HOOD' AKORESTON OIMOOGAN
Agamemnon was tricked and murdered
        TON PALAI EK DOLERAS ATHEOOTATA
that was a long time ago
        MATROS HALONT' APATAIS AGAMEMNONA
but a dirty hand did it, maternal,
        KAKA TE KHEIRI PRODOTON HOOS HO TADE
        POROON
and to breed their destruction
        OLOIT' EI MOI THEMIS TAD' AUDAN
if my deem is heard in dooming
        EI MOI THEMIS TAD' AUDAN

ELEKTRA:
    Yes, you are come nobly to help me,
    I can feel that,
    but I must go on.

    DEAD, he is dead, I must go on.
    It's my job,
    I have never asked to neglect it,
    let me go on alone.

CHORUS:
    But you won't get him back out of black hell
    by praying and groaning,
    you destroy yourself with too much of it,
    no harm to let up for a little.

(*emphatic and explicit with meaning to ram it in*)

    ALL OUTOI TON GEX AIDA
    PANGKOINOU LIMNAS PATER ANSTASEIS
    OUTE GOOIS OUTE EUXAIS

    Nothing to be DONE about it.

(CHORUS *trying to get idea into what they consider hysterical female*)

Why do you make it all the harder?

ELEKTRA:

It would be childish to forget him,
I'd be a ninny. Carried off that way
                a ITUN aien Itun.
I think my mind groans as the sound of Itys
lamenting, terrified,
bringing the news from Zeus.
Niobe weeping in a stone tomb
has a better portion from heaven,
weeping forever.
HAT EN TAPHOO PETRAIOO
AIAI DAKRUEIS.

CHORUS:

OUTOI SOI MOUNA TEKNON
AXOS EPHANE BROTOON
Not only you, dear,
everyman alive's got his load.

PROS HO TI SU TOON ENDON EI PERISSA
HOIS HOMOTHEN EI KAI GONA KSUNAIMOS
HOIA XRUSOTHEMIS DZOOEI KAI IPHIANASSA
Poor Chrysothemis, Iphianassa
and your boy brother
in exile
god send 'em back to Mycenae

KRUPTA T'AXEOON EN HAEBA
OLBIOS HON HA KLEINA
GA POTE MUKAENAIOON
DEKSETAI EUPATRIDAN DIOS EUPHRONI
BAEMATI MOLONTA TANDE GAN ORESTAN
Till Orestes come to the throne.

ELEKTRA:

Whom I keep on expecting,

9

childless, wretched,
unwed, in a dither of fear,
muddly with tears,
one thing after another, unending, and always worse;
and he's forgotten all
that's ever happened to him or been told him
every message I get is a cheat
always he wants to come
but never shows up.

CHORUS:
THARSEI MOI, THARSEI TEKNON
(*chorus moving / pause / move*)

ELEKTRA:
Gone, gone so much
hopeless and there's no help
wasted already, gone by in despair
no going back on that
fatherless, loverless, without stand-bye
housed neath my father's bed
kenneled and fed on trash
in a shapeless sack.

CHORUS:
She'd a gloomy voice when he came;
and a gloomy sound when the brass axe hit him,
on the couch there in his dining room.
A twisty idea
and a letch that killed him,
one vehemence led to another
procreating the form
whether god or man did it.

ELEKTRA:
That day was the vilest of all days
and that night at dinner was worse
                    beyond speakable language

10

horrible.
I saw my father killed by the pair of 'em
          watched himself being killed
and insulted.
Bitched my life, that did, that betrayal.
Zeus avenger, don't let 'em enjoy it unpunished.
Make it hurt. Them in their luxury! Agh!

CHORUS:
    Hush! Stop sounding off or talk sense.
    Quit piling troubles one on top of the other
    always making a row with that grouch of yours.
    Don't take the discussable to the powerful

    PSUXA POLEMOUS; TA DE TOIS DUNATOIS
    OUK ERISTA PLATHEIN.

    only gives 'em a handle.

ELEKTRA (*starts as if muttering*):
    DEIN EN DEINOIS ENANGASTHEN
    It's too horrible, I can't keep it in.
    I know you mean well, it's no use.
    Go way and leave me alone,
    let me have my cry out.

CHORUS:
    But, dearie, you make it all worse,
    I'm talkin' to you like a mother, you can trust me.

ELEKTRA:
    Is there any limit to the nature of misery?
    Is there anything pretty about neglecting the dead?
    Has that idea cropped up anywhere among men?
    If so I don't want their respect
    and if I come near to getting any good from it

11

may I not live tranquil among 'em
by smothering my keening for the shame of this house.
For if the dead lie down—earth and then nowt,
wretched
and there be no death for a death,
shame would go wrack,
all duty would end and be nothing.

CHORUS:

I rushed out here for your sake as well as mine,
if you don't like what I say, have it your own way,
we'll stick by you.

ELEKTRA:

I'm sorry, I oughtn't to let 'em get me down,
but I am driven to it,
they've got the power, all I can do is yammer
and make too much noise. Excuse it.
I'm ashamed of this clatter.
Could any decently brought up girl
see that done to her father, and act any different?
I see it day and night getting thicker, not dying down
and my own mother the most loathsome of all
and I have to live in the same house with
the people who murdered my father
and have 'em pushing me round
WHACK, take it, WHACK, leave it,
which ever way they've hexed it.

How do you think I pass my time anyhow?
When I see Aegisthus sitting there
in my father's chairs
even wearing his clothes
pouring libations
right by where he killed him
then havin' mother right there in the same bed
just to show off, a whore, a mother? Call it
a concubine

she's got so used to the dirty slob,
no longer scared of the curse,
celebrates with a dance one a month
with a whole sheep for "his dinner"
joke that is,
           but it gets me down all the same.
And I go moulder in an attic
and blubber over "Agamemnon's bean-o,"
the accursed feast named in his honor
yes, they call it by old pop's name.

Can't even have my cry out in peace
with that old big-talk bawling me out:

"You the only slut ever lost a father,
nobody else had any troubles,
go rot and keep on yowling in hell."

That's how she goes on, bubbles over
EXCEPT when someone says Orestes is comin'
then she gets scared and blows her top proper,
goes shoutin' frantic:

"You got him away, it's all your fault
you cheated me out of Orestes, you sneak,
mark my word,
you'll get your come-uppence."

that's her bark, and her ponce sicks her on
                    marvelous
of all the dastardly yellow pests
fightin' from under her skirts
and me rotting away, waiting here for Orestes
to put a stop to it all.
And he's worn out all hope, by waiting,
dither and dally,
yes, my dears, a nice place for moderation and decency
and with all this rot I've gone rotten.

CHORUS:
   HE, is Aegisthus here, while you're talkin'?

ELEKTRA:
   Naturally NOT. Think I could get out, with him in?

CHORUS:
   Well then I can say what I think.

ELEKTRA:
   He's out, you can say what you like.

CHORUS:
   Well about your brother, is he coming or not?

ELEKTRA:
   Sez he will an' he don't.

CHORUS:
   A man's likely to go slow, take his time, on a big job.

ELEKTRA:
   If I'd gone slow, he wouldn't be there to take it.

CHORUS:
   Hang on, he was born honest,
   he won't let you down, cares too much.

ELEKTRA:
   If I didn't think that, I'd be dead.

CHORUS:
   Sshh, here comes your sister.
   I see she's carrying . . . oh . . . offerings,
   like for DOWN THERE, all very proper.

CHRYSOTHEMIS (*tone of thorough weariness, and discouragement*):
   Oh Dear, are you out here again, sounding off,

14

never learn, makes it worse,
let out every fool feeling you got in your gizzard.
I don't like it any better than you do.
If I could get hold of the power, the levers
I'd show 'em what I think,
but for the present I'm going to keep in my sail
and not think I'm harming 'em when I'm not,

and I advise you to do the same.
Just the same I know you're right and
what I say isn't so, and what you think is,
but I've got to obey in order to keep my freedom of action.

ELEKTRA:
It's just awful the way you take her part
and forget him.
YOU didn't think of any of that,
it's just what she's told you.
You can do one of two things: be honest and speak out
or play dumb and forget your friends.

You just said if you had the power
you'd show 'em how you hate 'em
but when I'm out to do right by my father
will you come in on it? No, no you try to put me off it.
Need we add cowardice to all the rest of the filth? (*pause*)
Tell me, or lemme tell you what good it could do me
to stop objecting out loud.
I'm not dead yet, it's a dirty life
but my own.
It annoys 'em. That honors the dead
if the dead get any joy out of THAT.

You say you hate 'em, but
you play ball with our father's assassins.
Well I wouldn't knuckle under, not for one minute
nor for all this stuff they have given you

(*She takes hold of* CHRYSOTHEMIS' *bangles or bracelet or whatever ornament or fine dress*)

that you swank about in.
        Have your big dinners, comforts
and everything easy,
        your lie-down, flow-about life.
If I don't eat, I don't make myself spew with disgust.
Keep my self-respect anyhow.
I wouldn't want to have a sense of honor like yours
nor would you if you understood it.
You're even called by your mother's name
when you could use father's
        and he was some good,
best of the lot of 'em.
It don't look nice.
Most people would say you are going back
on your dead father, and the people you care for.

CHORUS:
   For the gods sake, keep your tempers,
   there's something to be said on both sides
   if either of you could learn from the other.

CHRYSOTHEMIS:
   Oh, I'm used to the way she goes on.
   I wouldn't have come here now, but she's in worse danger
   in fact should stop her howls once and for all.

ELEKTRA:
   Well what could be worse? If you tell me
   anything worse, I'll shut up.

CHRYSOTHEMIS:
   All I know is that if you don't quit bawling
   they'll shut you up where you'll never see daylight
   in some black jail outside the country,

do stop to think, and don't blame me
when it's too late.

ELEKTRA:
So that's what they're up to.

CHRYSOTHEMIS:
As soon as Aegisthus gets back.

ELEKTRA:
The sooner the better.

CHRYSOTHEMIS:
So he can??
You're off your poor head. What for?

ELEKTRA:
To get away from the lot of you
as far as possible.

CHRYSOTHEMIS:
But at least you're alive here?

ELEKTRA:
A beautiful life, something for me to admire!

CHRYSOTHEMIS:
Might have been if you'd learned to adjust yourself.

ELEKTRA:
Don't educate me up to double crossing friends.

CHRYSOTHEMIS:
I'm only telling you to bend and not break
when you come up against power.

ELEKTRA:
Slobber over 'em. Not my way.

17

CHRYSOTHEMIS:
  It's perfectly respectable not to fail
  out of sheer stupidity.

ELEKTRA:
  All right I'll fail, for my father's honor
  if it's so ordered.

CHRYSOTHEMIS:
  I am sure he'd excuse one.

ELEKTRA:
  You commend everything nasty.

CHRYSOTHEMIS:
  Well I suppose you won't listen to anything I say
  let alone agree with it.

ELEKTRA:
  Probably NOT . . . Not yet such a cipher.

CHRYSOTHEMIS:
  Well, I'll be moving along.

ELEKTRA (*noticing the offerings for the first time, having been up to now absorbed in her own fury*):
  Goin' far?
  Uh'uh. What you carrying THAT for,
                    all roasted?

CHRYSOTHEMIS:
  Mother told me to go water the grave.

ELEKTRA:
  What!! and nobody she hates worse?

CHRYSOTHEMIS:
  You mean the one she murdered.

18

ELEKTRA:
Where did she get THAT fancy? Whose idea was it?

CHRYSOTHEMIS:
Had a nightmare, I think, and it scared her.

ELEKTRA:
Gods help us. Whatever next!

CHRYSOTHEMIS:
That's cheered you up, now she's scared.

ELEKTRA:
You tell me about that dream, then I'll talk.

CHRYSOTHEMIS:
I don't really know that much about it.

ELEKTRA:
Spill it. A little word often counts for a lot,
up or down.

CHRYSOTHEMIS:
What they say is that it was like as if dad
stood there right by her, and a second time
in plain daylight. And took hold of his sceptre,
the one Aegisthus uses now, and planted it by the altar
and a branch grew right out of it
and spread all over Mycenae.

That's what one of the girls says, who was there
while she was telling it before Helios.
That's all I know except that she was so scared
she sent me out. Now listen
you pray to the gods. Don't be a fool,
listen to me, before it's too late.

ELEKTRA:

Don't put a bit of it on the tomb.
It's not clean before men or gods that you
plant gifts or carry lustrations
from that hating woman, to dirty his grave.
Throw 'em away, bury 'em, hide 'em deep,
so long as none of 'em gets near his grave.
Let 'em stay and wait for HER till she dies,
let her find 'em in hell, when she dies,
a little deposit.

The crust she's got, throwing her flowers and dirty water
onto him after bumping him off.

You think the dead from his grave is goin' to
reach up a lovin' right hand for these ornaments?

Killed like any damn foreigner
and wiped 'er bloody 'ands on his 'air,
cut off his hands and feet to keep the
ghost from walkin' and grabbin' her.

But don't YOU think of carrying that
stuff to purge her of murder.
Chuck it away.
Cut off the tip of one of your curls,
that makes a pretty gift,
and for me, god knows, I haven't anything,
I give my whole disheveled mop.
Here, take it,

(*jerks out a lock of her own (wig) violently*)

and my belt, it's not much,
just a plain belt without ornaments.
But kneel and beg him to come up out of the earth
to protect us

and that young Orestes get the upper hand of his enemies
and stay alive till he's got 'em under his feet,
so that we can crown him with something better
than we give now.

I think mebbe he's troubling her dreams.
Anyhow, you do this for me, and for him
even if he is dead, we still love him.

CHORUS:
    She's on the right track now, dear,
    you do what she says.

CHRYSOTHEMIS:
    I certainly will, it's what ought to be done
    and no point disputing it.
    But keep quiet about it for gods' sake,
    don't let mother get wind of it,
    if she does the old usurer will
    make me pay extra for the risk.

(*exits*)

CHORUS:
    You can say that I never guess right,
    a born fool without second sight,
    that my head was never screwed tight,
    but if Justice don't win just this once
    I'm a dunce

    and before a great time has gone by.
    My heart's risin' now
    and my dreams are breathin' deep
    with a free and airy sound:
    the greek king won't forget you,
    he'll be comin' yet
    and the double headed axe

21

be payin' back the smacks
and the bloody blood be flowin' once again.

And Vengeance will come out
from her hiding bush no doubt
with the rush of brazen shoes,
wid the sound of brazen shoes,
she will come with brazen tread
to their adulterous bed
to wipe out all the stain
as they wrestle there unwed;

ever with lock and sigh
ill doer and ill do's mate
shall never dodge out of fate,
ill done hath ill do won,
black ends that with black began,
fate shall out run any man,
fate is stronger than man, blacker than man.
Nothing foretells tomorrow to man
neither horrors in dream nor in oracles
if that night-sight don't damn well smash 'em.

(*Sing the Greek*)

> OO PELOPOS HA PROSTHEN
> POLUPONOS HIPPEIA
> HOS EMOLES AIANAES
> TADE GA. TADE GA.

(CHORUS LEADER *speaks*)

For Myrtil's curse
when he was drowned after that crooked horse-race,
chucked out of his gilded car into the sea
and the curse has continued
on the house of Pelops
rotting the earth.

ELEKTRA

KLYTEMNESTRA (*entering*):
Out here again making trouble, might have known it
now Aegisthus' not here,
he keeps you from making dirt on the family doorstep.
He's away and you pay no attention to me.
You've shot off a lot of brash talk
to a lot of people,
a lot more than was so
about how forward I am, how unjust
insulting you and your gang.

Nobody ever insulted me? Eh?
Bad? Eh?
Well I've heard 'em from you often enough
just as bad.
Your father, eh? that's your excuse
always that, never different.
I killed him, I did, yes me, have I ever denied it?
And a good job it was, don't I know it
with Justice on my side
as you'll have to admit if you think straight.

This "father" you're always crying about
was the only one of the Greeks who would stand for
sacrificing your own sister to the gods,
he didn't have as much trouble in makin' her as I had
he put her in, I got her out.

Well who did he sacrifice her FOR,
you tell me, for whom and for what?
The Greeks. You say for the Greeks?
which of the two Greeks was it?
It wasn't up to them to kill my girl
and if he killed her for his brother Menelaus
weren't there any rites due to me?

Hadn't Menelaus two children of his own?

23

Wasn't it up to them to die, if it was
their father and mother who were cause of the sailing?

Did Hell have more appetite for my children than hers?
Or had the rotter less paternal affection
than Menelaus?
Signs of a gutless and dirty father I say
they are, even if we split on it.

And it's not what your dead sister would say if she
could manage a voice.
I'm not peeved about what I've done
and if you want to sling abuse
try slinging it at somebody else in the family,
get on the right track. Put the blame where it belongs.

ELEKTRA (*calm*):
    Well this time you can't say I started it.
    But if you let me,
    I'll give you the rights of it about my father and sister.

KLYTEMNESTRA:
    Of course I'll let you. If you
    had always had that tone of voice
    no one would have objected to listening.

ELEKTRA:
    All right, you admit you killed him.
    Can anyone say anything worse?
    Legally or illegally,
    well justice didn't come into it.
    It was your letch for that bounder you're lying with.
    Go ask Artemis and her dogs why she
    shut up the winds in Aulis
    all of them, for what vengeance?
    And as she won't tell you, I will.
    He was hunting away thru her forest

and not only started a spotted buck with 8 points
but made smutty jokes about it, it was
a kill
not according to the hunting rites.
And Artemis didn't like it,
she held up the Achaeans
to make my father pay
for the buck with his own daughter.
That's why and how she was killed,
she went to the altar smokes
a sacrifice,
the troops couldn't get either home or to Ilion
no other way out.
He did it against his own nature
not in favor of Menelaus.

But even if he had done it for Menelaus,
to take it your way,
ought you to have killed him?
What law was that?
You'd better be careful setting up that sort of law
for the rest of the world, you'll get into trouble
and wish you hadn't.
For if blood for blood makes justice,
you'll be the first to go.
But look, is all your talk sophistry,
fake, fake, a mere sophistry?
Say what you like, you get into bed with the murderer
and breed to put out the true heirs,
expect me to like that?
Call that avenging a daughter? Is that your excuse?
A dirty job to marry an enemy
for the sake of a daughter?
And nobody allowed to warn you
without your putting up a squawk about a slandering mama.
Slave-driver more than a mother I'd call you,

and a rotten life I have with you and your fellow-feeder,
you're always putting all the low jobs onto me.

And poor Orestes who got away by the skin of his teeth
wearing away in misery
you always accuse me of saving him
to come back and cleanup the dirt you've done here
and you know damn well I would have too, if I could.
So if I'm a dirty scold, abusive,
completely impudent,
looks like it runs in the family,
not likely to disgrace your temperament.
I got it all from you.

CHORUS:
  Gheez, she's a-goin' at it fierce,
  right or not she don't care a hang.

KLYTEMNESTRA:
  Why should I bother what she thinks
  spittin out at her mother that way, at her age?
  By god there's nothing she'd stop at,
  no sign of shame.

ELEKTRA (*suddenly perfectly calm*):
  Well now I think I have got a sense of shame.
  I distinguish between suitable conduct
  and what I'm driven to by your hate and your devilments.
  Dirty workers teach dirty work.

KLYTEMNESTRA:
  You beastly whelp, it's what I've said
  and NOT done, that makes you talk a great deal too much.

ELEKTRA:
  Now you're talkin',

you did the job, not me,
and things done get names.

KLYTEMNESTRA:
  By the Virgin you'll pay for this
  when Aegisthus gets home.

ELEKTRA:
  Nice nature, comin' out, ain't it?
  Temperamental, tells me to say what I like
  and hasn't got brains enough to hear it.

KLYTEMNESTRA:
  You'd even spoil the sacrifice, shouting,
  now I've let you get it all out.

ELEKTRA (*coldly*):
  Go along, yes, DO sacrifice, please
  and don't say my noise is jinxing you,
  I won't say anything more.

KLYTEMNESTRA (*to maid*):
  Here, you pick up all this fruit and incense
  so I can pray and get rid of these worries.

  (*sotto voce*)

  Hear me Apollo, Patron,
  keep down this scandal
  (I am not speaking among friends,
  she is ready to yatter
  and spread silly nonsense all thru the town,
  envious little bitch).
  But do hear me, let me explain
  this ghost in the shifty vision of a dream.
  O Apollo Lykeios, if it's lucky let the luck come to me
  and if it's evil, let it fall to my enemies,

27

if anybody's trying to cheat me out of my money
don't let 'em.
Let me run the house of Atreides as long as I live
and keep hold of the sceptre. Preserve me
to live comfortably with these friends,
and with children who like me
and who aren't gone bitter with spite and gloom.

O Phoibos Lykeios hear me, with favor,
give to us all that we ask,
and you know all the rest I don't say
for the sons of God see all that there is.

(*enter the* TUTOR)

TUTOR:
   I'm a stranger in these parts, can
   any of you kind ladies tell me
   if that's Milord Aegisthus's palace?

CHORUS:
   Yes, stranger, you've hit it, bullseye.

TUTOR:
   Would I be right in sayin' that woman there is the queen?
   She looks it.

CHORUS:
   She's it.

TUTOR:
   Gruss Gott, your highness, I've got good
   news for you and Aegisthus, come from a friend of his.

KLYTEMNESTRA:
   That's nice. (*dropping voice*)
   Wonder who the deuce that can be.

28

TUTOR:
Phanoteus, of Phocia. It's a serious matter.

KLYTEMNESTRA:
Well, what is it? Go on, stranger,
must be good if it comes from him.

TUTOR:
Orestes is dead. That's the short of it.

ELEKTRA:
Oooh, that's the end. I'm finished.

KLYTEMNESTRA:
What, what, don't bother with her.

TUTOR:
He's dead, Orestes, finished! na poo.

ELEKTRA:
Ruin, ruin, I can't go on.

KLYTEMNESTRA:
(*to* ELEKTRA) Mind your own business.
Now, stranger, tell me about it,
how did it happen?

TUTOR:
That's what I'm here for.
He went up for the big Delphic prize.
That's the biggest Greek games
and when he heard the herald yellin' out the first race,
the foot race, he come out shining
admired of all beholders
an' he got the proize uv the first race.
I never see a man like him, from start to finish,
the crown he had for the victory,

I'm only tellin' part of it.
He took all the foive proizes, you could hear the umpires
tellin' it: Agamemnon's son, young Orestes.
Win for Argos. Old general's son licked the lot of 'em.

(*change tone, and shaking head*)

There's no lickin' the god's bad temper.
An' the next day toward sundown
he entered, there were all the charioteers,
Sparta, Achaia, and two boys from Libya:
drivers, and one team of Thessalian mares;
an Aetolian, young chestnut fillies, and another from Megara.
A white Aneian, and the Athenian, number nine,
the city the gods put up, and last and tenth the Beotian.
And the umpires ranged 'em up as the lot fell
and they sounded off with the brazen horn
shakin' the reins and a-lickin' the horses
and a-yellin' till you couldn't hear over the plain
and the track wuz narrow, the lot of 'em drivin' togedder
and a-lammin' the horses, each one tryin' to git out of
the bunches
and the wheels a-rollin', and the horses a-snortin'
and their sweat spattered over the cars,
and their breath steamin' on the droivers in front of 'em
and Orestes come round at the turn, at the turns
all of 'em, shavin' the pillars
loosin' the off horse and pullin' in on the nigh.
And the Aneian's bolted between the sixth and seventh round
and foul'd the Barcaen's, and they all piled up then
the lot of 'em
except the Athenian
                    who slowed up
and then Orestes
                    pulled in on his team
nothin' left but the two of 'em,
all RIGHT, till the very last turn, when his

axle-tip hit the pillar
                    and busted
and he got t'rown over the rail
and caught in the reins of his horses
                    wid the crowd yellin' for pity
now seein' him bumped on the ground and now lifted
wid his feet in the air
                    till the other charioteers
got hold of his horses
and found him
broke beyond recognition,
his best friend wouldn't have known him. (*pause*)
And the Phoceans burnt him then and there on the pyre
and the envoys are comin', bringin' what's left in an urn
to lay his dust in his fatherland.
It's a sad story, madam, I
saw it wid my own eyes.
Never a worse one.

CHORUS:
                    PHEU, PHEU, MISERA.
Ah, ah, that's the end of the dynasty!
                    TO PAN DE DESPOTAISI TOIS PALAI
They are blotted out root and branch.
                    PRORRISDON HOOS EOIKEN EPHTHARTAI
                    GENOS.

KLYTEMNESTRA:
Oh god, what, which, I dunno if it's lucky.
Terrible, it's terrible, it's, it's useful anyhow.
It's a miserable state of things when
nothing but my own sorrows save my life.

TUTOR:
What, lady, am I gettin' you down with this news?

KLYTEMNESTRA:
That's the worst of being a mother,

can't hate a child no matter how badly they treat you.

TUTOR:
Seems I came on a useless errand.

KLYTEMNESTRA:
No, not useless, if you've got proof of his death
born of my life, forgetful of the breasts that suckled him
banished himself to get away from me
never seen me since he left the country
accused me of killing his father
he was threatening terrible
what awful things he would do
till I couldn't get a night's sleep or a cat nap
thinking I was going to die every minute
and, now, eh, now I needn't be scared of him any more
nor of that worse little bloodsucker living here with me,
the pest,
now we'll get a day's peace somewhere
in spite of her threats.

ELEKTRA:
Ooooh, he's dead and it fits her book
miserly, motherly excitement
very pretty.

KLYTEMNESTRA:
Not for you. I dare say he's better off.

ELEKTRA:
Holy vengeance, god hear her,
and him not cold in the grave.

KLYTEMNESTRA:
Fate HAS heard, and managed it very nicely.

ELEKTRA:
Go on, keep it up. You're top dog, you've

hit the jackpot.

KLYTEMNESTRA:
You and Orestes can't spoil it now.

ELEKTRA:
Spoil it! No, this is OUR finish.

KLYTEMNESTRA (*to* TUTOR):
You'd deserve more than a good fat tip
if you'd make her hush and finish her yatter.

TUROT:
Well ma'am, I'll be goin', if everything is in good shape.

KLYTEMNESTRA:
NO, no, can't treat a friend's messenger that way.
Come in, do, and let her yowl
out here about her friends' troubles, and hers.

(KLYTEMNESTRA *and* TUTOR *exit*)

ELEKTRA:
Looks like she's grief-stricken, weepin' an' wailin'
about her poor son being wiped out that way?
Went out bursting with laughter.
                              Poor me
OO TALAIN EGO
ORESTA PHILTATH HOOS M'APOOLESAS THANOON
                    not ever
I'll lie down
at the gate here
and die here,
got no friends.
And if anybody kills me, because he don't like it,
any of them inside, be a favor, that killing,

got no wish to live anyhow.

CHORUS:
God, where the hell are you? Zeus,
Apollo, no light and no lightning.
Is there no one to show these things up?

ELEKTRA:
AI AI

CHORUS:
No use crying.

ELEKTRA:
AIH

CHORUS:
SHHH.

ELEKTRA:
You are killing me.

CHORUS:
What?

ELEKTRA:
Don't tell me about life after death,
that's only another kick when I'm down.
They're dead and gone forever.

CHORUS (*sings softly? trying to comfort her*):
OIDA GAR ANAKT' AMPHIAREOON KHRUSODETOIS
   HERKESI
KRUPHTHENTA GUNAIKOON
KAI NUUN HUPO GAIAS
Nay but King Amphiarion
that died for a golden chain

caught in a false wife's net
under the earth reigns yet.

ELEKTRA (*disgusted and bored with song*):
Ajhh

CHORUS (*singing*):
He reigns and lords his mind.
PAMPSUKOS ANASSEI

ELEKTRA (*beginning to cheer up, still dubious, but singing now and echoing
the tone of the Chorus*):
AHI

CHORUS:
And bodes no good at all
for her who slew him.

ELEKTRA:
Slain.

CHORUS:
Ay, slain.

ELEKTRA:
Known, o'er known
mid grief, an avenger.
I have none.
He was, and is not,
vanished away, torn from me.

CHORUS:
Sorrow attains thee, sorrow.

ELEKTRA:
Known, don't know, over known,
day after day, moon over moon,

overfull, pain over pain,
horrors of hate abate not
ever.

CHORUS:
Our eyes be witness.

ELEKTRA:
Then do not deceive me
neither lead me astray.

CHORUS:
Thou sayest?

ELEKTRA:
Not into emptiness
                where there is no one
at all.

CHORUS (*the two "alls" simultaneously*):
All men must die.

ELEKTRA:
But to die so, so clawed in whirling doom
torn in the track, if so that death must come

CHORUS:
mid tortures so
whose death was unforeseen.

ELEKTRA:
How not? and him so far
no hand to lay

CHORUS:
                AHI

ELEKTRA:
  His mangled limbs
  in decent grave
  unwept to meet strange clay?

CHORUS:
  AHI! PAPAI!

CHRYSOTHEMIS (*trots in puffing*):
  Oh dearest . . . . . so happy . . . . . . such news . . . .
  I'm all out of breath from running. . . .
  your troubles are over.

ELEKTRA (*voice of complete skeptical weariness*):
  What? You with a cure-all?

(*after a pause, looking her up and down*)

  Where did you find what ain't?

CHRYSOTHEMIS:
  He's here. Orestes is here.
  I'm telling you, just as sure as you see me.

ELEKTRA:
  You're CRAZY, poor dear, plumb crazy,
  don't joke about horrors.

CHRYSOTHEMIS:
  I'm not, I swear by the hearth-stone
  he's come for the two of us.

ELEKTRA (*sighs*):
  Oh dear, poor dear, has anyone LIVING
  put that nonsense into your head?

CHRYSOTHEMIS:
  No, but me, ME, from what I've seen,
  me, with my own eyes, seen.

37

ELEKTRA:
 WHAT proof? you poor fool
 you're blotto delirious.

CHRYSOTHEMIS:
 For gods' sake wait till I finish telling you
 and then decide whether I'm batty.

ELEKTRA:
 All right, go on, if you like to talk.

CHRYSOTHEMIS:
 It was like this:
 I was goin' to father's old grave
 and there was milk newly splashed over it
 running down from the top of the mound
 and all sorts of wreaths all around it
 out there for father
 like as if
 and I was wondering, and looking to see who,
 who on earth could,
 as if someone might be coming

(ELEKTRA *masked, at first not even looking at* CHRYSOTHEMIS *but boredly into distance, gradually grows attentive. Slowness in turning of head, as per Noh*)

 and when I saw everything quiet
 I sneaked up nearer the mound
 and there was a new lock of hair on it
 right on the edge
 and, oh dear, it come over me while I was looking at it
 that ORESTES had put it there,
 almost as if I had seen him
 and I picked it up and burst out crying, I was so happy,
 it can't be an ill omen,

and I'm perfectly sure nobody else could have put it there,
who'd have cared except us?
I didn't and you didn't
cause you couldn't get out of the house,
SHE wouldn't have, she's not taken that way
and she couldn't have, without being seen.
No, no, no, my dear, Orestes put that stuff in the grave,
you can buck up now.
The same devils can't always run things,
ours have been pretty bad,
but the luck's changing,
happen a really good day might come in.

ELEKTRA:
Poor thing, you were always soft in the head.

CHRYSOTHEMIS:
But aren't you glad?

ELEKTRA:
You don't know whether you're on earth, or raving.

CHRYSOTHEMIS:
Don't know what I've seen with my own eyes, SEEN.

ELEKTRA:
He's dead, and the dead won't help you, and he can't,
god help you, poor you.

CHRYSOTHEMIS:
Oh, o, o, but who told you.

ELEKTRA:
A man who was there and saw it. Killed.

CHRYSOTHEMIS (*in tone of complete puzzlement*):
Where is he, the man? It's very peculiar.

ELEKTRA:

In THERE, and mother's so glad to see him.

CHRYSOTHEMIS:

Oh dear . . . But whoever can have put all those wreaths on the tomb?

ELEKTRA:

Somebody must have put 'em there for Orestes.

CHRYSOTHEMIS:

O, O, and me running to make you happy
and not knowing we'd only come into more trouble
besides what we had.

ELEKTRA:

Well that's how it is. And now you turn to and help me
at least this much with the load.

CHRYSOTHEMIS:

You want me to raise the dead?

ELEKTRA:

That's not what I said. At least I wasn't born crazy.

CHRYSOTHEMIS:

Well what do you want me to do,
that I can do?

ELEKTRA:

Don't break down,
and do what I tell you.

CHRYSOTHEMIS:

I'll do anything that can be the least use.

ELEKTRA:

You can't do a good job without work.

40

CHRYSOTHEMIS:
I know that. I'll do anything I can.

ELEKTRA:
Well then listen.
I'm going to finish it up.
We got no more friends to stand by us.
Hell's grabbed the lot
and left us
you can see that, nobody left but us.
As long as HE was alive I went on
hoping he'd come and put things right about father,
wipe out the murder.
Now he's gone, not there any more,
I rely on you,
I hope you won't hold back,
we've got to kill Aegisthus ourselves,
you're not scared?
It's our father was murdered,
we've only got our own hands,
might as well look at it straight,
here you are crying and grousing about being cheated out
of father's fortune, well here it is:
and we're not getting any younger
without a man and unmarried,
and without a room of your own,
home of your own,
unbedded, unchambered.
Don't think they'll ever let you get married.
Aegisthus won't let us have children,
he's too cagey for that,
not to put him out of the running.
But you do what I tell you.
FIRST you'd be showin' respect for your dead father down
under
AND for your brother as well.
SECONDLY you could live like a free woman, free born,

as you were,
for the rest of your life,
and you'd get a man fit to marry.
People recognize quality, everybody does.
You listen to me, and we'd both get respected,
anybody from here or abroad would say:

"There they are, those girls saved the dynasty,
risked their lives doing it,
threw out the crooks, settled the murderers' hash.
You just got to like 'em,
everybody's got to respect 'em."

(*dreamy half-tranced voice*)

We'd have our proper place of honor
in processions and in assemblies
on account of our courage.
We'd have a reputation everywhere
and it would last even when we are dead.

Trust me, my dear, and stand by your father,
work with me for your brother,
get me out of my misery,
get yourself out of yours,
and remember this, the free born ought not to
sink into slavery.

CHORUS:
Well I guess
lookin' forward is about the best ally one could
have, if you're talking or listening
to things like this.

CHRYSOTHEMIS:
No, girls, if she weren't on the wrong track
she'd have had a little caution before she sounded off

and she just hasn't got any.

(*to* ELEKTRA)

Where do you look to get the nerve to fight
or get me into the ranks?
Can't you see you were born a woman not a man?
You haven't got the physical strength
of these people you're up against.
Their gods, their luck is comin' up every day
and ours going out, not comin' in at all.

(CHRYSOTHEMIS *repetitive and very patient*)

You try to break a man like that?
Who could get away with it
unharmed,
and not make a complete mess of it.
Don't make it worse,
if anybody heard you talkin' this way
you'd get into more trouble,
we won't get OUT of anything that way,
and fine talk's no use if we're dirty dead.
Death's not the worst that can happen
but not to be able to die when you want to.
I put it to you, before we're completely wiped out
us two and all of the family
keep your temper, hold in.
I'll keep my mouth shut about what you've said
cause I think it's, all of it, useless.

But do hang onto your wits, from now on.
Don't go up against people in power.

CHORUS (*to* ELEKTRA):
You better listen, there's nothing more useful
to a human being than forethought and a prudent mind.

43

ELEKTRA:
Just as I thought . . .
All right, I'll do it alone,
it's got to be done,
have a try at it anyhow.

CHRYSOTHEMIS:
Oooh Lord
I wish you'd taken the chance
the day he died!
Anything was possible then.

ELEKTRA:
Not that I didn't want to; I hadn't the sense.

CHRYSOTHEMIS:
I wish you still had as much.

ELEKTRA:
That means you won't help me at all.

CHRYSOTHEMIS:
It CAN'T be lucky.

ELEKTRA:
Nice mind, no guts!

CHRYSOTHEMIS:
I can bear up even under that compliment.

ELEKTRA:
You won't have to stand any more.

CHRYSOTHEMIS (*blandly*):
That remains to be seen.

ELEKTRA:
Oh get out, you're no use at all.

CHRYSOTHEMIS:
I am so, but you can't see it.

ELEKTRA:
Go tell it all to Mama.

CHRYSOTHEMIS (*explanatory*):
But I don't hate you that way.

ELEKTRA:
No, but think how you'd lead me to shame.

CHRYSOTHEMIS:
No I would NOT.
I'm only asking you think forward.

ELEKTRA:
And accept YOUR values?

CHRYSOTHEMIS:
When you get untangled, I'll take to yours,
you can think for us both, then.

ELEKTRA:
That's talking, too bad you mean it the wrong way on.

CHRYSOTHEMIS:
That's just the trouble with you.

ELEKTRA:
What? You mean what I say isn't perfectly true?

CHRYSOTHEMIS:
EVEN JUSTICE CAN BE A PEST.

ELEKTRA:
Anyhow, I don't want to go by your standards of conduct.
I'd rather die.

45

CHRYSOTHEMIS:
But if you did, you'd probably find I'm right.

ELEKTRA:
I'm going on anyhow, you can't scare me.

CHRYSOTHEMIS (*very soberly*):
You're serious? You won't think it over?

ELEKTRA:
Nothing stinks worse than bad advice.

CHRYSOTHEMIS:
You just don't understand what I'm saying.

ELEKTRA:
This isn't something that's just come into my head.

CHRYSOTHEMIS (*resignedly*):
Well, I'll go now.
You can't stand my talk, and I don't think
you're going the right way about it.

ELEKTRA:
Yes, go along, but I'll never trail after you
for the urging.
It's useless to chase after shadows,

(*mezzo voce, as if reflecting*)

such a lot of them,
all of them void.

CHRYSOTHEMIS:
If you ever aim to teach yourself to think straight,
think about it now. For my words will come back too late . . .
late.

CHORUS:

TI TOUS ANOOTHEN PHRONIMOOTATOUS
  OIOONOUS
ESOROOMENOI TROPHAS KAEDOMENOUS APH
  OON
TE BLASTOOSIN APH OON TONASIN
  HEUROOSI
TAD OUK EP' ISAS TELOUMEN.
ALL' OU TAN DIOS ASTRAPAN
KAI TAN OURANIAN THEMIN
DARON OUK APONAETOI
OO KHTHONIA BROTOISI PHAMA,
KATA MOI BOASON OIKTRAN
OPA TOIS ENERTH' ATREIDAIS,
AXOREUTA PHEROUS' ONEIDAE

Shall not justice be done
By Zeus among men?
Shall a sound be borne under earth
to the sons of Atreus?
  All is not well in his hall.
  His line dies out.
  HOTI SPHIN AEDAE TA MEN EK DOMOON
    NOSEI
  DAE TA DE PROS TEKNOON DIPLAE
  PHULOPIS OUKET EKSISOUTAI

From above
wise birds of omen
to be observed,
tossed and alone
Elektra mourns,
constant aid hath she none.
As Philomel in grief
her sire's shade
so shamed of all the world
nor cares to live or die
were he avenged.

47

A child, indeed, of what race!
What breed! Nor would she live in shame.

OUDEIS TOON AGATHOON
OO PAI PAI

So fame's all-hovering wing
shall bear her praise
for beauty of heart and mind
for constant faith.

Nay, ere she die
may power come
to lift her high,
may yet her house be strong
as Zeus gave law.

(*Enter* ORESTES *and* PYLADES)

ORESTES:
Eh, can any of you ladies tell me:
did we hear right and
are we getting to where we wanted to come to?

CHORUS (*more or less automatically, mechanically answering*):
Where do you want to come to?
AND WHY?
What are you here for?

ORESTES:
Aegisthus. Where does he live?

(*with morgue and double entente*)

I've been looking for him for SOME time.

CHORUS (*gruffly*):
Well yuh can't blame the fellow that told you.

(*thumb over shoulder, pointing*)

You got here.
This is it.

ORESTES:
Well, eh, will any of you go in and, eh,
say politely that we have respectfully got here
eh . . . on foot.

CHORUS:
This unfortunate girl should.
She's of the family.

ORESTES (*dubiously, accent and tone a bit grim and deliberate*):
Yes, lady? Would you go say that some Phocians
have come for Aegisthus?

ELEKTRA (*half-sob*):
Oh God, I spose you've got the proof with you.

ORESTES:
Proof of what? Old Stroffy
told us to bring the news of Orestes.

ELEKTRA (*sort of gasp*):
Eeh, I was afraid so

(*in sort of glaze noticing her own hands*)

I'm all of a tremble.

ORESTES:
We've got it here, all that is left of him
in this little jug, as you can see if you want to.

ELEKTRA:
  O. O It's all all I can bear.

ORESTES:
  If it's Orestes you're crying for,
  if it's for his troubles
  he's all there in the urn.

ELEKTRA:
  Oh give it to me, for god's sake, give it to ME.

(*hardly pause, but spoken staccato during the clauses*)

  It's the end of the line.
  We're all there together:
  ashes.

(ELEKTRA *clutching at the urn which Pylades is carrying*):

ORESTES:
  Give it to her, let her have it, whoever she is
                                                  a gift
  she's not asking from spite,
  must be a friend or one of the household.

            ELEKTRA'S KEENING:
  All that is left me
  my hope was Orestes
  dust is returned me
  in my hands nothing, dust that is all of him,
  flower that went forth.

  Would I had died then
  ere stealing thee from the slaughter
  died both together
  lain with our father.

Far from they homeland
died far in exile
no hand was near thee
to soothe thy passing
corpse unanointed
fire consumed thee
all now is nothing
strangers have brought thee
small in this urn here
sorrow upon me
fruitless my caring.

I as mother and sister both
thy nurse also ere thou hadst thy growth
this was my past
and swept away with thee
ever to me
thy summons came.

All in a day
and is no more.

Dead Agamemnon, dead now my brother,
I am dead also, the great wind in passing
bears us together.
Mirth for our foemen.

(*anger now stronger than grief, for a moment: spoken*)

And that bitch of a mother is laughing
and they haven't sent back even the shape of him,
but a ghost that can't do its job.

Ajnn, ajnn.

Thou the avenger, no more avenging

born to misfortune, ashes avail not
shadows avail not.
Ahi, ahi,
bodiless
brother that art not.

(*spoken*)

The spirits love me no longer.
You kept sending messages
secretly, you would take vengeance.

(*sings*)

Thy death, my dying
dread road thou goest
brother, my slayer

(*singing to the urn*)

Oimoi! Oimoi!

Take me in with you
I now am nothing, make place beside thee
naught into naught, zero to zero
to enter beside thee
our fortune equal
death endeth pain.

CHORUS:
Mortal thy father, all men are mortal.
Mortal Orestes,
all men must die.

ORESTES:
I can't stand much more of this.

ELEKTRA:
What's it to you?

ORESTES:
Good god. Are you Elektra?

ELEKTRA:
I am, and in misery.

ORESTES:
Heaven help me.

ELEKTRA:
What do you care about me?

ORESTES (*very quick & angry*):
What in hell have they done to you?

ELEKTRA:
But are you sorry for ME ?

ORESTES:
Unmarried, and such a life.

ELEKTRA:
What are you lookin' at?
What you got to be sad about?
It isn't YOUR funeral.

ORESTES:
I didn't know the half of it.

ELEKTRA:
What has that got to do with ANYTHING?

ORESTES:
Seeing you in this condition . . .

ELEKTRA

ELEKTRA:
You haven't seen anything yet.

ORESTES:
Amn't I seeing enough, can there be anything more, more, worse?

ELEKTRA:
Yes, living here with these assassins.

ORESTES:
Whose assassins?

ELEKTRA (*patiently and being explicit*):
My father's, and me a slave.

ORESTES:
Who compels you?

ELEKTRA:
They say she's my mother.

ORESTES:
How? Beats you? Starves you?

ELEKTRA:
Yes, and everything else.

ORESTES:
And there's no one to help you, or stop her?

ELEKTRA:
Nobody. Nothing but the dust you've got there.

ORESTES:
Poor dear, I've been sorry for you, a long time.

54

ELEKTRA:
Well you're the first man that ever WAS
and the only one.

ORESTES:
Cause I've got the same trouble.

ELEKTRA:
You mean you're a relative?

ORESTES:
Can you trust these people?

ELEKTRA:
They're all right. You can trust 'em.

ORESTES:
Give me back that jug, and I'll tell you.

ELEKTRA:
No, don't cheat me that way, for gods' sake.

ORESTES:
Come on, you won't miss it.

ELEKTRA:
Oh gosh, don't take it, it's all I've got,
don't rob me.

ORESTES:
I won't. Give it here.

ELEKTRA:
Oh poor Orestes, if I can't even bury you.

ORESTES:
Watch what you're saying.
You oughtn't to weep.

ELEKTRA:
What when my brother's dead.

ORESTES:
You oughtn't to talk that way about him.

ELEKTRA:
What! Amn't I fit to?

ORESTES (*admiringly*):
You're fit for anything, but that isn't your job.

ELEKTRA:
Not when I'm carrying his body here in my hands?

ORESTES:
They're not his. That's a fairy tale.

ELEKTRA:
Well where IS his grave.

ORESTES:
It ain't. You don't bury people while they're still alive.

ELEKTRA:
What are you talking about?

ORESTES:
Only the truth.

ELEKTRA:
He's alive?

ORESTES:
As I am.

ELEKTRA:
YOU?

ORESTES:
Here's dad's ring.

ELEKTRA:
OO PHILATON PHOOS

ORESTES:
What a day; I'll say it is.

ELEKTRA:
And I hear you talking.

ORESTES:
Yes. We're agreed on that.

ELEKTRA:
And I can hold onto you.

ORESTES:
Never let go.

ELEKTRA:
Oh my dears, this is Orestes.
He wasn't really dead after all.
He was just pretending, so he could get here.

CHORUS:
Yes we can see him. Makes one cry this does.

ELEKTRA:
Heart, heart, heart thou art come.

ORESTES:
Yes, but keep quiet,
for a bit just keep quiet.

ELEKTRA:
What for?

ORESTES:
Somebody might hear there inside.

ELEKTRA (*sings Greek like Carmagnole. THIS song can be burst into. Like wild Sioux injun war dance with tommy hawks*):
ALL OU MA TEN ARTEMIN
ADMAETAON AIEN
ARTEMIN
HOTOTOTOI
Clear again, not to be ended
not to be forgotten
how our ill started, trouble began.

ORESTES:
By god when the women get goin' it's Mars.

ELEKTRA:
Oh to hell with all the hens
in the old hen house.

I ain't afraid of hens
cause they ain't a bit of use.

ORESTES:
Don't I know it but
to tell it in its time
when the DEED recalls it.

ELEKTRA:
Any time's right, now, I've hardly got my mouth free.

ORESTES:
I'll say it is. And you damn well keep it free.

ELEKTRA:
How?

ORESTES:

By not talking too much at the wrong time.

ELEKTRA:

You came when I'd given up hope.
I got to keep quiet now?

ORESTES:

I came as the gods moved me.

ELEKTRA:

That's the best the gods have done yet.

ORESTES:

I don't want to stop down your enjoyment
but afraid you're overdoing it.

ELEKTRA:

Oh a long time to the right road
you "deign" (gosh) deign to show up here
but not me seeing me full of toil
DON'T . . .

ORESTES:

Don't what?

ELEKTRA:

Don't defraud me
of the pleasure of seeing you here.

ORESTES:

Damn well let anybody else try it.

ELEKTRA:

You don't mind?

ORESTES:
Of course not, how could I?

ELEKTRA:
You like it?

ORESTES:
Sure I'll do what you tell me, why not?

ELEKTRA (*performing for chorus*):

> Oh dearest friends
> if now's to ear
> a voice I ne'er
> had hoped to hear
>
> If joy shall not
> burst forth at this
> then ever dumb in wretchedness
> should one live on in deep distress.
>
> Now thou art here
> in full daylight
> I shall not pour
> forth my delight,
> who ne'er in deepest woe
> had forgot thee.

ORESTES (*trying to stop her, gently, by covering her mouth*):
Yes, yes, but lay off the talk.
You don't have to tell me how that bitch and Aegisthus
are running all dad's place to ruin
sluicin' it out in extravagance, luxury,
no time for all that,
got to get on with the job.
Tell me the best way to get to it

so I can fit the time,
where to show, and where to hide
to put an end to these bumptious bastids, and how.

And don't look so damn happy
that when we go in, she'll twig something is up.

Keep your face mum, keep on weepin' and bawlin'
so she won't guess what we're up to,
and laugh when we've finished the business
and have got to some sort of freedom.

ELEKTRA (*breathlessly eager*):
Ye'ss my dear, I just love it,
it's all yours and not mine,
I won't get in the way, I won't bother.
What you like, I like, and my
pleasure's from you not me, and I wouldn't
pain you the least little bit for anything in
the world cause it would run counter to the
good luck now running.
You know Aegisthus is out, she's alone in the house.
Don't worry about my lookin' happy.
I loathe her, and I've been weeping and crying
(for joy, but she needn't know that)
for the dead come alive
to do what I never believed
so incredible that if father himself should come
here alive I'd believe it,
since you got here this way.
Tell me what you want done and I'll follow
since even alone I have done one or two things
and I'd have damn well thrown 'em out
or gone bust, been decently dead.

ORESTES (*puts hand over her mouth*):

But HUSH
sounds as if someone
was coming out.

ELEKTRA:
  Yes, gentlemen, this is the way
  nobody in this house will object to what you're bringing in.

(TUTOR *enters*)

TUTOR (*furious*):
  You BLOODY fools shut up.
  Ain't you got ANY sense whatever?
  No more care for your lives?
  You ain't on the brink of trouble,
  you are plumb bang in the middle.
  Don't you know you're in danger
  real danger, damn it.
  If I hadn't been there keepin' watch in this doorway
  they'd already know what you're at before you get
  to it, before you get in there yourselves.

  I've saved you that, anyhow,
  and now if you've got thru with your gabble
  your blasted roaring exuberance
  go in, but quiet,
  no good wasting time, either,
  get it over.

ORESTES:
  What does it look like in there?

TUTOR:
  All jake, especially since no one knows you.

ORESTES:
  You've told 'em I'm dead?

ELEKTRA

TUTOR:
You're a ghost in hell as far as they go.

ORESTES:
And they're DEElighted.
What do they say about that?

TUTOR:
We'll go into THAT later.
The worse they do, the better . . .

ELEKTRA:
For god's sake, who's this?

ORESTES:
Can't you see?

ELEKTRA:
Haven't the foggiest . . .

ORESTES:
Well you handed me over to him.

ELEKTRA:
What, what?

ORESTES:
Well he sneaked me out of here
and got me to Phocis.

ELEKTRA (*gasps*):
The only one of the lot
who stood by me when father was murdered.

ORESTES:
That's him. Now hush.

ELEKTRA (*to* TUTOR):
                    What a day!

You've done it alone.
You've saved the line.
How did you get here?
You've saved him and me
in all this misery, bless your hand.

(*grabs 'em, and presses them to her booZUM or cheeks*)

Oh gods bless the feet that brought you.

(*bit hysterical still*)

How could you go on and not tell me,
and telling us all of those lies
and yet brought him.
You seem more like a father,
OHHH how I hated you.
What a dear.

TUTOR:
Yes, yes, but now hush.
There's enough history to fill nights and days.
We can go into that when the time comes.

(*then noticing* ORESTES *and* PYLADES *are still standing there*)

What the hell are you doing here?
Get with it, she's alone,
if you lose time, she'll have all the slaves up to fight you,
not only the servants but the palace guards,
the whole corps of them,
and no pikers.

ORESTES (*to* PYLADES, *who hasn't said a damn word*):
Come on, Pylades, cut the cackle.
May the gods of the door be with us.

(*Exit* ORESTES *and* PYLADES)

ELEKTRA (*does the praying/ sings, sort of sing-song*):
> O King Apollo
> HILEOOS
> Favor us, favor us,
> oft have I prayed thee,
> my little I gave thee,
> Phoibos, Lukeios,
> aid the right now,
> let the gods show their god head.

CHORUS:

Mars breathing blood
hounds that never miss their prey
miss never their spring, under the roof,
seeking the doers of all ill, by stealth, and by guile,
Mars breatheth blood,
avenging dogs that never miss their prey,
ineluctable, enter the palace roof,
not long to wait for the proof of my presage.
Will, heart, and all.

ELEKTRA (*emerging from the door, or slowly turning as part of a pivoted door*):
> Oh my dears, my dears . . .
> It's coming . . .
> sh hh hhh

CHORUS:
What! What!
whatarethey doing?

ELEKTRA:
She's putting the wreath on the urn . . .
and . . . and they're waiting.

CHORUS:
Whatchu come out for?

ELEKTRA:
To keep watch for Aegisthus
so he don't catch 'em.

KLYTEMNESTRA:
AIHII, nobody left,
oohhh assassins.

ELEKTRA:
Hear that? Yes, dears, it's a noise.

CHORUS:
It's awful. Gimmee the creeps.

KLYTEMNESTRA:
Aaaah, Aegisthus. AE-GIS-THUS.

ELEKTRA:
Hear it, that's it again.

KLYTEMNESTRA:
Pity your mother.

ORESTES (*grim*):
Did you pity father or me?

CHORUS (*now sings cry of misery keening on one note or minimum rise and fall but monotonous and legato*):
O city, o WRETCHED house
and the curse's tooth gnaws
day after day.

KLYTEMNESTRA:
That's done it.

ELEKTRA:
Hit her again.

KLYTEMNESTRA:
  Twice
  twice
  always twice.

ELEKTRA (*between her teeth*):
  Ajh. GOD I wish it was Aegisthus.

CHORUS:
  Aah!
  Curses work out. They live who lie under ground.
  The blood of the dead, long dead
  overwhelms their slayers
  and the dead hands
  drip Mars, and the slain
  blood, blood. I can't blame 'em.

ELEKTRA:
  Orestes! How are you?

ORESTES:
  All right, the house is clean again, if what Apollo said
  is right.

ELEKTRA:
  The bitch is dead?

ORESTES (*sobered tone vs.* ELEKTRA'S *exultation*):
  You won't have any more trouble with mother.

CHORUS:
  Ssshhh. Here comes Aegisthus.

ELEKTRA:
  Back, can't you get back!

67

ORESTES:
Where is the bloke?

ELEKTRA:
Comin' up from the lower town, very chesty . . .

CHORUS:
Quick, get into that vestibule. Hop!
Good job so far. Now the next one.

ORESTES:
We'll do it, don't worry.

ELEKTRA:
Hurry, hurry.

ORESTES:
Exit.

(*He leaves.*)

ELEKTRA:
Now mine.

CHORUS:
Now just a few polite words would come in handy,
so he won't guess he's rushin' plumb bang into ruin
an' he damn well deserves it.

AEGISTHUS (*enters, flanked by body guards?*):
Say you, where can I find these chappies from Phocis?
They say that Orestes got killed in a chariot race
all messed up.

(*to* ELEKTRA)

Here YOU, always so full of lip,

it's mostly your business,
                    you ought to know.

ELEKTRA:
  Sure I know. Think I don't care
  about the last relative left me?

AEGISTHUS:
  Well where are these chaps? Spit it out.

ELEKTRA:
  Inside, and she's SO pleased to see 'em.

AEGISTHUS:
  They said he was dead? How do they know?

ELEKTRA:
  They don't. They've only got the corpse with 'em.

AEGISTHUS:
  Can I get a look at it?

ELEKTRA:
  Yes (*slight pause*), yes (*spoken softly*):
  It's an awful mess.

AEGISTHUS:
  'Tain't often you say anything to please me.

ELEKTRA:
  Go on and enjoy it, if that's the kind of thing you enjoy.

AEGISTHUS:
  Shut up.

(*to* CHORUS)

  Get these doors open

so everyone in Mycenae, and Argos
can see.

(*they open the big portone doors, slowly*)

If anybody had hopes of this man
they can now see him dead

(*smacks his thigh*)

and do what I tell 'em
and not wait till they're dead to find out.

ELEKTRA:
Oh, I've learned that.
No use goin' up against people in power.

(ORESTES *enters with the body of* KLYTEMNESTRA, *covered*)

AEGISTHUS:
O Zeus, I see a sight not sent without envy,
looks as if the gods didn't like him!
Here, I take that back, it ain't lucky.
Lift that napkin off his face, I'm one of the family
in mourning.

ORESTES:
Lift it yourself. It's not my place
to show these signs of love and affection.

AEGISTHUS:
That's right.

(*to* ELEKTRA)
                    Go call Klytemnestra
if she's at home.

ORESTES (*as* AEGISTHUS *lifts napkin*):
 She's right there. You needn't look any further.

AEGISTHUS:
 GAaaaaaa!

ORESTES:
 Whazza matter? Haven't you seen her before?

AEGISTHUS (*in fury*):
 Who th' HELL. Damn damn
 I'm trapped.

ORESTES:
 Haven't
   you
     ever
       learned
 that the
    DEAD
      don't
        DIE?

AEGISTHUS:
 Ajh. You're Orestes.

ORESTES:
 Ain't you clever. And it took you so LONG to find out.

AEGISTHUS:
 Here now, wait a minute, just let me . . .

ELEKTRA:
 DON'T
  Don't let him get a word in,

the brute's caught, what good's a half hour?
Kill him. Kill him.
    And let the sextons cart him out,
get the stuff out of sight,
    and let me forget it.

ORESTES (*snarling*):
  GET ON IN THERE, stow the gab,
  you're in for it.

AEGISTHUS (*breaking*):
  Why have I got to go in
    and die in the dark?
  Why can't you do it here?

ORESTES:
  None of your business. You'll die
  where you killed my father.

AEGISTHUS:
  Fate, fate, under this damned roof of Pelops
  everything happens here.

ORESTES:
  You'll get YOURS here at any rate.
  I can tell you that much.

AEGISTHUS:
  You didn't get that from your father.

ORESTES:
  Make a song about it?

AEGISTHUS:
  I follow.

ORESTES (*patient, dragging voice, but sword pointing in small of A's back*):
  After you.

AEGISTHUS:
  Hah. 'Fraid I'll give you the slip?

ORESTES:
  No, but you aren't dying for pleasure.
  You've got to go through with it ALL.
  It's a pity you can't all of you die like this
  and as quickly, every one like you.
  It would save a lot of unpleasantness.

CHORUS:

      O SPERM ATREOOS
          Atreides, Atreides,
    come through the dark.

My god, it's come with a rush!

      DELIVERED, DELIVERED
      SWIFT END
         SO SOON
         TE NUN TELEOOTHEN.

Pronunciation of Selected Greek
Vowels and Consonants

Consonants	Pronunciation
D	English "do"
SD	English "wisdom"
TH	English "top" (emphatically pronounced)
PH	English "pot" (emphatically pronounced)
KH	English "cat" (emphatically pronounced)
R	Scottish rolled "r"

Vowels	
E	English "pet"
EI	English "fiancée," German "Beet"
EU	Cockney "belt," Italian "eulogia"
AE	English "hairy," French "tête"
O	English "pot"

Vowels	Pronunciation
OO	English "saw"
OI	English "boy"
OU	English "too"
U	French "ruse"

Double Consonants	
PP	English "hip-pocket"

Double Consonants	**Pronunciation**
TT	English "rat-trap"
SS	English "disservice"
LL	English "wholly" (contrast "holy")

Literal Translations of Greek Phrases

Prepared in collaboration with
Marina Kotzomani

p. 5
IOO MOI MOI DUSTAENOS
woe me me wretched

p. 6
OO PHAOS AGNON
Oh holy light

THRENOON OODAS
POLLAS D'ANTEREIS AESTHOU
How many keening songs have you known?
How many straight dealt blows?

p. 7
ALL' OU MEN DE
LAEXOO THRENOON
But I swear I will not stop lamenting

OO DOOM AIDOU
OO KHTHONI HERMAE
Oh House of Hades
Oh Hermes of the underworld

HAI TOUS ADIKOOS THNAESKNONTAS HORATH
HAI TOUS EUNAS HUPOKLEPTOMENOUS
ELTHET ARAEXATE
You [Furies] who see those dying unjustly,
You who see those whose beds are stolen,
Come, help us

pp. 7–8
OO PAI PAI DUSTANOTATAS
ELEKTRA MATROS TIN AEI
TAKEIS HOOD' AKORESTON OIMOOGAN
TON PALAI EK DOLERAS ATHEOOTATA
MATROS HALONT' APATAIS AGAMEMNONA
KAKA TE KHEIRI PRODOTON HOOS HO TADE POROON
OLOIT' EI MOI THEMIS TAD' AUDAN
EI MOI THEMIS TAD' AUDAN
Oh child, child of a most wretched
mother, Elektra. Why are you always
pining such a ceaseless lamentation
for Agamemnon who long ago
was godlessly trapped by the deceits
of your treacherous mother
and was betrayed by an evil hand.
May he who has contrived these things
perish, if I may lawfully say it.

ALL OUTOI TON GEX AIDA
PANGKOINOU LIMNAS PATER ANSTASEIS
OUTE GOOIS OUTE EUXAIS
But you won't indeed rouse your father
from the all-receptive lake of death
neither by groans nor by prayers.

p. 9
HAT EN TAPHOO PETRAIOO
AIAI DAKRUEIS
You who weep forever in a rocky grave

OUTOI SOI MOUNA TEKNON
AXOS EPHANE BROTOON
You are not the only mortal child
to whom this grief has come

PROS HO TI SU TOON ENDON EI PERISSA
HOIS HOMOTHEN EI KAI GONA KSUNAIMOS

HOIA XRUSOTHEMIS DZOOEI KAI IPHIANASSA
Your grief exceeds the grief of those living in your house,
of those of your kin and blood.
See how Chrysothemis lives and Iphianassa

KRUPTA T'AXEOON EN HAEBA
OLBIOS HON HA KLEINA
GA POTE MUKAENAIOON
DEKSETAI EUPATRIDAN DIOS EUPHRONI
BAEMATI MOLONTA TANDE GAN ORESTAN
(and Orestes) hidden from sorrows, happy in his youth,
someday the famous land of Mycenae will welcome
back noble Orestes, coming to this land with
Godsent favorable step

p. 10
THARSEI MOI, THARSEI TEKNON
Courage, child

p. 11
PSUXA POLEMOUS; TA DE TOIS DUNATOIS
OUK ERISTA PLATHEIN
(Always breeding) wars in your soul; one cannot
fight with the powerful

DEIN EN DEINOIS ENANGASTHEN
I have been compelled to do terrible things in terrible
circumstances.

p. 22
OO PELOPOS HA PROSTHEN
POLUPONOS HIPPEIA
HOS EMOLES AIANAES
TADE GA. TADE GA.
Ancient horsemanship of Pelops, loaded
with pain, how wearisome you have proved
to this land

p. 31
PHEU PHEU MISERA

TO PAN DE DESPOTAISI TOIS PALAI
PRORRISDON HOOS EOIKEN EPHTHARTAI GENOS
The whole of the ancient family of our lords, indeed,
the dynasty, has perished, it seems, root and branch

p. 33
OO TALAIN EGO
ORESTA PHILTATH HOOS M'APOOLESAS THANOON
O wretched me.
Orestes, dearest, your death has destroyed me.

pp. 34–35
OIDA GAR ANAKT' AMPHIAREOON KHRUSODETOIS HERKESI
KRUPHTHENTA GUNAIKOON
KAI NUUN HUPO GAIAS
PAMPSUXOS ANASSEI
King Amphiaraus, as I know, was caught in women's
golden snares and now beneath the earth
he reigns over all the souls.

p. 47
TI TOUS ANOOTHEN PHRONIMOOTATOUS OIOONOUS
ESOROOMENOI TROPHAS KAEDOMENOUS APH OON
TE BLASTOOSIN APH OON TONASIN HEUROOSI
TAD OUK EP' ISAS TELOUMEN.
ALL'OU TAN DIOS ASTRAPAN
KAI TAN OURANIAN THEMIN
DARON OUK APONAETOI
OO KHTHONIA BROTOISI PHAMA,
KATA MOI BOASON OIKTRAN
OPA TOIS ENERTH' ATREIDAIS
AXOREUTA PHEROUS' ONEIDAE
Why, when we see the most prudent birds on high
caring for the nurture of those from whom
they are sprung and from whom they derive
benefit, do we not do the same?
But, by the lightning-bolt of Zeus and
Themis, who rules high in the sky,
they are not long untroubled. Ah rumor

that holds on earth amongst mortals, cry
out for my sake the pitiable tidings to
the Atreidae beneath the earth, bearing
them shames that bear no celebration.

HOTI SPHIN AEDAE TA MEN EK DOMOON NOSEI
DAE TA DE PROS TEKNOON DIPLAE
PHULOPIS OUKET EKSISOUTAI
(Rumor, tell them) that now their house is sick,
their two children are in an irreconcilable conflict.

p. 48
OUDEIS TOON AGATHOON
OO PAI PAI
Nobody knows those who are good
Oh child child

p. 57
OO PHILATON PHOOS
Oh dearest light

p. 58
ALL OU MA TEN ARTEMIN
ADMAETAON AIEN
HOTOTOTOI
But by the
ever-virgin Artemis
Hooooray!

p. 65
HILEOOS
gracious

p. 73
O SPERM ATREOOS
TE NUN [HORMAE] TELEOOTHEN
Oh the race of Atreus
was completed today with force

New Directions Paperbooks—A Partial Listing

For complete listing request free catalog from
New Directions, 80 Eighth Avenue, New York 10011

†Bilingual

For complete listing request free catalog from
New Directions, 80 Eighth Avenue, New York 10011   †Bilingual